Work Smart:

Drop Your Hard Work

AND

Boost Productivity

JAMES K. WEIL

Chapter 1: Introduction

- Definition of "working smart"
- Overview of the book's content
- Why working smart is important

Part I: Understanding Your Work

Chapter 2: Defining Your Goals and Priorities

- Setting SMART goals
- Identifying and prioritizing tasks
- Creating a schedule that aligns with your goals and priorities

Chapter 3: Identifying Your Strengths and Weaknesses

- Conducting a personal SWOT analysis
- Capitalizing on your strengths
- Addressing your weaknesses

Chapter 4: Delegating and Outsourcing

- Identifying tasks that can be delegated or outsourced
- Finding the right people for the job
- Communicating effectively with others

Part II: Improving Your Productivity

Chapter 5: Time Management

- Techniques for managing your time effectively
- Avoiding time-wasters and distractions
- Maintaining focus and concentration

Chapter 6: Automation and Technology

- Tools and software to automate and streamline tasks
- Integrating technology into your workflow
- Tips for using technology productively

Chapter 7: Learning and Personal Development

- Importance of continuous learning and development
- Strategies for acquiring new skills and knowledge
- Overcoming barriers to learning

Part III: Cultivating Habits for Success

Chapter 8: Mindset and Attitude

- Cultivating a growth mindset
- Developing a positive attitude towards work
- Overcoming negative self-talk and limiting beliefs

Chapter 9: Health and Wellness

- Importance of taking care of your physical and mental health
- Strategies for improving your diet and exercise
- Techniques for managing stress and preventing burnout

Chapter 10: Building Relationships

- Importance of networking and building relationships
- Strategies for building and maintaining professional relationships
- Leveraging your network for success

Chapter 11: Conclusion

- Summary of the book's content
- Final thoughts on working smart
- Action steps for implementing what you've learned.

CHAPTER 1

Introduction

Work is an essential part of our lives, and it plays a crucial role in our personal and professional development. At its core, work is the effort we put into achieving a particular goal or outcome. It can take many different forms, including paid employment, volunteering, or pursuing a personal passion.

Work provides us with a sense of purpose and identity, and it allows us to contribute to society and make a difference in the world. It also helps us develop valuable skills and experiences that can benefit us in both our personal and professional lives.

However, work can also be challenging and stressful, and it can sometimes feel overwhelming or unfulfilling. That's why it's essential to approach work with a positive and proactive mindset, focusing on strategies and techniques that can help us work smarter, not harder.

Throughout this book, we will explore different ways to enhance productivity and efficiency, reduce stress and burnout, and cultivate habits and attitudes that promote success and well-being in the workplace. Whether you're a seasoned professional or just starting your career, this book is designed to provide you with practical tips, strategies, and insights to help you achieve your goals and reach your full potential in the world of work.

Definition of "working smart"

"Working smart" refers to the practice of optimizing one's time and effort to achieve maximum productivity and efficiency. It involves working in a strategic and focused manner, prioritizing tasks, and leveraging tools and techniques that streamline work processes and minimize wasted effort.

Working smart is not about working longer hours or putting in more effort; instead, it's about working in a way that allows you to achieve your goals while maintaining a healthy work-life balance. This requires a combination of time management, task prioritization, delegation, automation, and personal development.

By working smart, individuals can increase their productivity, reduce stress and burnout, and achieve better outcomes in both their personal and professional lives.

Overview of the book's content

The book "Working Smart: How to Drop Your Hard Work and Boost Productivity" is divided into three parts, each focusing on different aspects of working smart.

Part I: Understanding Your Work In this section, readers will learn how to define their goals and priorities, identify their strengths and weaknesses, and delegate tasks effectively.

They will discover how to create a schedule that aligns with their goals and priorities, and how to communicate effectively with others.

Part II: Improving Your Productivity This section is all about enhancing productivity and efficiency by managing time effectively, leveraging technology and automation, and continuously learning and developing new skills. Readers will learn how to avoid time-wasters and distractions, use technology productively, and adopt a growth mindset.

Part III: Cultivating Habits for Success The final section of the book focuses on cultivating habits and attitudes that promote success and well-being in the workplace. Readers will discover the importance of maintaining physical and mental health, building relationships, and leveraging their network for success. They will also learn how to develop a positive attitude towards work and overcome negative self-talk and limiting beliefs.

Throughout the book, readers will find practical tips, strategies, and exercises to help them implement the concepts and techniques discussed in each chapter. By the end of the book, readers will have a comprehensive understanding of how to work smart, reduce stress and burnout, and achieve their goals with maximum efficiency and effectiveness.

Why working smart is important

Working smart is important for several reasons:

1. Increased productivity: By working smart, individuals can optimize their time and effort, enabling them to accomplish more tasks in less time. This translates to increased productivity and efficiency, which can lead to higher job satisfaction and better outcomes.
2. Reduced stress and burnout: Working smart involves prioritizing tasks, delegating responsibilities, and taking breaks. This helps to reduce stress and prevent burnout, allowing individuals to maintain a healthy work-life balance.
3. Improved quality of work: By focusing on high-priority tasks and leveraging tools and techniques that streamline work processes, individuals can produce higher-quality work that meets or exceeds expectations.
4. Career advancement: Working smart can help individuals stand out in the workplace, demonstrating their value and potential to employers. This can lead to career advancement opportunities and increased earning potential.
5. Personal development: By continuously learning and developing new skills, individuals can expand their knowledge and expertise, which can lead to personal growth and increased confidence.

Overall, working smart is essential for achieving success in the workplace and maintaining a healthy work-life balance. It enables individuals to optimize their time and effort, reduce stress and burnout, and achieve their goals with maximum efficiency and effectiveness.

PART I: Understanding Your Work

Understanding your work is an essential aspect of working smart. It involves gaining clarity on your goals, priorities, strengths, and weaknesses, and aligning your efforts accordingly. Here are some key components of understanding your work:

1. Defining your goals: It's important to define your short-term and long-term goals, both personal and professional. This will help you prioritize your tasks and ensure that your efforts align with your desired outcomes.
2. Identifying your priorities: Determine which tasks are most critical to achieving your goals and prioritize them accordingly. This will help you avoid wasting time and effort on low-priority tasks that don't contribute to your desired outcomes.
3. Identifying your strengths and weaknesses: Knowing your strengths and weaknesses allows you to delegate tasks effectively, focus on areas where you excel, and develop strategies to improve areas where you need to grow.
4. Delegating tasks: Delegation is an important skill that enables you to leverage the strengths and expertise of others while focusing your own efforts on high-priority tasks. Be clear about your expectations and provide support and guidance to those you delegate to.
5. Communicating effectively: Communication is key to understanding your work and collaborating effectively with others. Be clear and concise in your communication, actively listen to others, and provide constructive feedback when necessary.

Overall, understanding your work is about gaining clarity on your goals, priorities, strengths, and weaknesses, and aligning your efforts accordingly. By doing so, you can ensure that you're focusing your time and effort on tasks that contribute to your desired outcomes and achieving maximum efficiency and effectiveness in the workplace.

CHAPTER 2

Defining Your Goals and Priorities

Defining your goals and priorities is a critical step in working smart. By setting clear goals and priorities, you can focus your efforts on tasks that are most important and relevant to achieving your desired outcomes. Here are some key tips for defining your goals and priorities:

1. Determine your long-term vision: Start by defining your long-term vision, both personally and professionally. What do you want to achieve in the long run, and how does that align with your values and passions?
2. Break down your vision into achievable goals: Once you have a long-term vision, break it down into smaller, achievable goals. This will help you create a roadmap for achieving your vision and provide a sense of direction.
3. Prioritize your goals: Not all goals are created equal, so it's important to prioritize them. Identify which goals are most important and relevant to achieving your long-term vision and focus your efforts on those.
4. Set specific, measurable, and achievable goals: When setting goals, make sure they are specific, measurable, and achievable. This will help you track your progress and ensure that you're making meaningful progress towards your desired outcomes.

5. Review and adjust your goals regularly: Goals should be reviewed and adjusted regularly based on changing circumstances and priorities. This will help you stay on track and ensure that you're always working towards what's most important.

Overall, defining your goals and priorities is a crucial step in working smart. It helps you focus your efforts on tasks that are most relevant to achieving your desired outcomes, and provides a sense of direction and purpose in your work. By setting clear, achievable goals and regularly reviewing and adjusting them, you can achieve maximum efficiency and effectiveness in the workplace.

Setting SMART goals

Setting SMART goals is a framework that can help you set clear, specific, and achievable goals. SMART is an acronym that stands for:

1. Specific: Your goal should be clear and specific, so you know exactly what you're trying to achieve. It should answer questions like who, what, when, where, and why.
2. Measurable: Your goal should be measurable, so you can track your progress and determine whether you've achieved it or not. This could involve setting a target number, percentage, or other quantifiable measure of success.
3. Achievable: Your goal should be achievable, taking into account your skills, resources, and constraints. It should be

challenging enough to motivate you, but not so difficult that it's impossible to achieve.

4. Relevant: Your goal should be relevant to your long-term vision, values, and priorities. It should align with your personal and professional aspirations and contribute to your overall growth and development.
5. Time-bound: Your goal should be time-bound, with a specific deadline or timeline for completion. This will help you stay focused and motivated, and ensure that you're making progress towards your desired outcomes.

Here's an example of a SMART goal:

Specific: Increase sales revenue by 10% in the next quarter by implementing a new marketing campaign.

Measurable: Track sales revenue on a weekly basis and measure progress against the 10% target.

Achievable: The 10% increase is achievable based on historical data and market trends, and the resources and skills needed for the new marketing campaign are available.

Relevant: Increasing sales revenue aligns with the company's overall goals and objectives, and contributes to long-term growth and sustainability.

Time-bound: The goal has a specific deadline of the next quarter, with milestones and deadlines established for each step of the marketing campaign.

Overall, setting SMART goals can help you focus your efforts, track your progress, and achieve your desired outcomes in a strategic and effective way.

Identifying and prioritizing tasks

Identifying and prioritizing tasks is a critical step in working smart. Here are some tips to help you identify and prioritize your tasks effectively:

1. Create a task list: Start by creating a list of all the tasks you need to complete. This will help you get a clear overview of what needs to be done.
2. Categorize your tasks: Categorize your tasks by level of importance and urgency. For example, you might categorize tasks as high, medium, or low priority, based on their impact on your goals and deadlines.
3. Evaluate the consequences of not completing a task: Consider the consequences of not completing a task. Will it impact your goals or deadlines? Will it lead to negative consequences?
4. Use the Eisenhower Matrix: The Eisenhower Matrix is a popular tool for prioritizing tasks based on importance and urgency. It involves categorizing tasks as urgent and important, important but not urgent, urgent but not important, or not urgent and not important.
5. Consider your energy levels: Consider your energy levels and prioritize tasks accordingly. For example, if you have more energy in the morning, prioritize important tasks that require more focus and concentration during that time.

6. Break down larger tasks into smaller ones: Break down larger tasks into smaller, more manageable tasks. This will help you make progress towards larger goals and stay motivated.
7. Review and adjust regularly: Regularly review and adjust your task list based on changing circumstances and priorities. This will help you stay on track and ensure that you're always working towards what's most important.

By identifying and prioritizing tasks effectively, you can focus your efforts on what's most important, stay organized, and achieve maximum efficiency and effectiveness in the workplace.

Creating a schedule that aligns with your goals and priorities

Creating a schedule that aligns with your goals and priorities is essential to working smart. Here are some steps you can take to create a schedule that works for you:

1. Identify your most important goals: Start by identifying your most important goals and priorities. What are the things that you absolutely must accomplish in order to achieve success in your work?
2. Estimate the time required for each task: Once you have identified your most important goals, estimate the amount of time required for each task. Be realistic in your estimates and account for any potential roadblocks or unexpected delays.

3. Break down larger tasks into smaller ones: If you have larger tasks that require significant amounts of time, break them down into smaller, more manageable tasks. This will make it easier to schedule and complete them.
4. Prioritize your tasks: Based on your goals and priorities, prioritize your tasks in order of importance. This will help you determine which tasks to complete first and how much time to allocate to each one.
5. Allocate time in your schedule: Once you have prioritized your tasks, allocate time in your schedule for each one. Be sure to leave some buffer time in case unexpected tasks or issues arise.
6. Schedule your most important tasks during your most productive time: Schedule your most important tasks during the time of day when you are most productive and focused. This will help you work efficiently and achieve the best results.
7. Regularly review and adjust your schedule: Regularly review your schedule and adjust it as needed based on changing priorities, deadlines, or other factors.

By creating a schedule that aligns with your goals and priorities, you can work more efficiently and effectively, and make progress towards your most important objectives.

CHAPTER3

Identifying Your Strengths and Weaknesses

Identifying your strengths and weaknesses is an important step towards working smart. Here are some tips to help you identify your strengths and weaknesses:

1. Reflect on your past experiences: Reflect on your past experiences and identify the tasks and projects that you excelled at. What were the tasks that came easily to you and that you enjoyed doing? What were the tasks that were more challenging and that you struggled with?
2. Seek feedback from others: Seek feedback from colleagues, supervisors, or mentors who can provide an objective perspective on your strengths and weaknesses. This can be especially helpful if you are looking for areas of improvement.
3. Take personality and skills assessments: There are a variety of personality and skills assessments available that can help you identify your strengths and weaknesses. These assessments can help you gain insights into your personality traits, work style, and areas where you excel or need improvement.
4. Identify your passions and interests: Identify the tasks and activities that you are most passionate about and enjoy doing. These can be strong indicators of your strengths and areas of expertise.

5. Analyze your performance data: Analyze performance data, such as productivity metrics, project outcomes, or customer feedback, to identify areas where you excel and areas that need improvement.

By identifying your strengths and weaknesses, you can focus on leveraging your strengths and improving your weaknesses to achieve maximum effectiveness and productivity in the workplace.

Conducting a personal SWOT analysis

A personal SWOT analysis is a tool that can help you identify your strengths, weaknesses, opportunities, and threats. Here are some steps you can take to conduct a personal SWOT analysis:

1. Identify your strengths: List down your strengths, such as skills, knowledge, and experiences that give you an advantage in your work. Think about what you are good at and what sets you apart from others.
2. Identify your weaknesses: List down your weaknesses, such as skills, knowledge, or experiences that need improvement. Think about the areas where you struggle or have received feedback for improvement.
3. Identify your opportunities: List down your opportunities, such as trends, advancements in technology, or new projects, that can help you achieve your goals. Think about the opportunities that you can capitalize on to enhance your career.

4. Identify your threats: List down your threats, such as competition, economic changes, or other challenges that can hinder your career growth. Think about the potential obstacles that can impact your success.
5. Analyze your SWOT: Review your SWOT analysis and identify the connections between your strengths, weaknesses, opportunities, and threats. Use this information to develop a plan to leverage your strengths, address your weaknesses, capitalize on opportunities, and mitigate threats.

By conducting a personal SWOT analysis, you can gain a deeper understanding of yourself and your career prospects. This can help you make informed decisions, develop a strategic plan, and achieve your career goals.

Capitalizing on your strengths

Capitalizing on your strengths is an important step towards working smart. Here are some tips to help you capitalize on your strengths:

1. Identify your strengths: As discussed earlier, you can use various methods to identify your strengths, such as self-reflection, feedback from others, personality and skills assessments, and performance data.
2. Focus on your strengths: Once you have identified your strengths, focus on leveraging them to achieve your goals. For example, if you are good at public speaking, seek opportunities to speak at conferences or events to showcase your skills.

3. Build on your strengths: Continue to develop your strengths by learning new skills or taking on new challenges that can help you enhance your expertise. This can help you stay competitive and relevant in your field.
4. Collaborate with others: Collaborate with others who have complementary strengths to yours. By working with others who have different strengths, you can create a more well-rounded team and achieve better outcomes.
5. Communicate your strengths: Communicate your strengths to others, such as your colleagues, supervisors, or clients. This can help you build your reputation and increase your visibility in the workplace.

By capitalizing on your strengths, you can increase your productivity, achieve better outcomes, and enhance your career prospects.

Addressing your weaknesses

Addressing your weaknesses is another important step towards working smart. Here are some tips to help you address your weaknesses:

1. Identify your weaknesses: As discussed earlier, you can use various methods to identify your weaknesses, such as self-reflection, feedback from others, personality and skills assessments, and performance data.
2. Create a plan: Once you have identified your weaknesses, create a plan to address them. This may involve taking courses, seeking mentorship, or practicing new skills.

3. Seek feedback: Seek feedback from others who can help you address your weaknesses. This may include colleagues, supervisors, or mentors who can provide guidance and support.
4. Set goals: Set specific, measurable, achievable, relevant, and time-bound (SMART) goals to address your weaknesses. This can help you track your progress and stay motivated.
5. Practice regularly: Practice regularly to develop new skills and address your weaknesses. This can involve role-playing, simulations, or real-life scenarios that allow you to practice and apply your new skills.

By addressing your weaknesses, you can enhance your capabilities, increase your confidence, and become more effective in your work. Remember, no one is perfect, and everyone has areas for improvement. The key is to acknowledge your weaknesses and take steps to address them.

CHAPTER 4

Delegating and Outsourcing

Delegating and outsourcing are important strategies to help you work smart. Here are some tips to help you delegate and outsource effectively:

1. Identify tasks to delegate: Identify tasks that are time-consuming or outside your area of expertise. These tasks can be delegated to others who have the necessary skills and knowledge.
2. Choose the right person: Choose the right person to delegate the task to. This may involve considering their skills, experience, and workload.
3. Provide clear instructions: Provide clear instructions to the person you are delegating the task to. This may involve explaining the task, setting deadlines, and providing necessary resources.
4. Monitor progress: Monitor the progress of the task to ensure it is completed on time and to the desired quality. This may involve setting up regular check-ins or progress reports.
5. Outsource strategically: Consider outsourcing tasks to external service providers who have specialized expertise or resources. This can help you save time and money while getting high-quality results.
6. Evaluate outcomes: Evaluate the outcomes of delegated or outsourced tasks to ensure they meet your expectations.

This can help you make informed decisions about future delegations or outsourcing.

By delegating and outsourcing tasks, you can focus on your strengths and priorities while leveraging the skills and resources of others. This can help you work more efficiently and effectively, and achieve better outcomes.

Identifying tasks that can be delegated or outsourced

Identifying tasks that can be delegated or outsourced is an important step towards working smart. Here are some tips to help you identify tasks that can be delegated or outsourced:

1. Identify time-consuming tasks: Identify tasks that take up a lot of your time but can be completed by someone else with less expertise or knowledge. Examples include administrative tasks, data entry, or routine customer service tasks.
2. Determine non-core activities: Determine non-core activities that are not essential to your business operations. Examples include bookkeeping, IT maintenance, or social media management.
3. Consider specialized expertise: Consider tasks that require specialized expertise or skills that are not available within your organization. Examples include graphic design, content writing, or legal services.
4. Evaluate cost-effectiveness: Evaluate the cost-effectiveness of delegating or outsourcing a task. Consider the time and

resources required to complete the task in-house versus outsourcing or delegating it to an external service provider.

5. Assess workload: Assess your workload and determine which tasks can be delegated to others within your organization. This can help you free up time and focus on high-priority tasks.

By identifying tasks that can be delegated or outsourced, you can work more efficiently and effectively while leveraging the skills and resources of others. This can help you achieve better outcomes and increase your productivity.

Finding the right people for the job

Finding the right people for the job is critical to successfully delegating or outsourcing tasks. Here are some tips to help you find the right people for the job:

1. Determine the required skills and expertise: Determine the skills and expertise required to complete the task successfully. This can help you identify potential candidates who possess the necessary skills and knowledge.
2. Use your network: Use your professional network to identify potential candidates who have the required skills and expertise. This may involve reaching out to colleagues, industry associations, or professional networks.
3. Advertise the job: Advertise the job on online job boards, social media, or other relevant platforms. This can help you attract a larger pool of potential candidates.

4. Screen candidates: Screen potential candidates to ensure they have the necessary qualifications and experience. This may involve reviewing resumes, conducting phone or video interviews, or administering skills tests.
5. Check references: Check references to verify the candidate's experience and qualifications. This can help you confirm that the candidate is a good fit for the job.
6. Communicate expectations: Communicate your expectations clearly to the candidate. This may involve setting deadlines, providing clear instructions, and outlining the desired outcomes.

By finding the right people for the job, you can ensure that delegated or outsourced tasks are completed successfully and to the desired quality. This can help you work more efficiently and effectively while leveraging the skills and resources of others.

Communicating effectively with others

Communicating effectively with others is essential for working smart. Here are some tips to help you communicate effectively with others:

1. Be clear and concise: Be clear and concise in your communication. Avoid using complex language or technical jargon that may be difficult for others to understand.
2. Listen actively: Listen actively to what others have to say. This can help you understand their perspective and identify potential areas of misunderstanding.

3. Ask questions: Ask questions to clarify any ambiguity or confusion. This can help you ensure that everyone is on the same page and working towards the same goals.
4. Use visual aids: Use visual aids such as diagrams, charts, or graphs to help convey complex ideas or data. This can help make your message more engaging and easier to understand.
5. Provide feedback: Provide feedback to others on their performance or work. This can help them understand what they are doing well and identify areas for improvement.
6. Be respectful: Be respectful of others and their opinions. Avoid using derogatory or offensive language that may be perceived as disrespectful.
7. Use appropriate communication channels: Use appropriate communication channels such as email, phone, or in-person meetings depending on the nature of the message and the audience.

By communicating effectively with others, you can build stronger relationships, minimize misunderstandings, and achieve better outcomes. This can help you work more efficiently and effectively while leveraging the skills and resources of others.

PART II

Improving Your Productivity

Improving your productivity is critical to working smart. Here are some tips to help you improve your productivity:

1. Eliminate distractions: Eliminate distractions such as social media, email notifications, or other interruptions that can break your concentration and disrupt your workflow.
2. Prioritize tasks: Prioritize tasks based on their importance and urgency. This can help you focus on the tasks that have the greatest impact on your goals and objectives.
3. Use time management techniques: Use time management techniques such as the Pomodoro Technique or the Eisenhower Matrix to help you manage your time more effectively.
4. Take breaks: Take breaks to help you maintain focus and avoid burnout. This can help you recharge your energy and improve your overall productivity.
5. Automate repetitive tasks: Automate repetitive tasks such as data entry or report generation to help you save time and increase efficiency.
6. Use productivity tools: Use productivity tools such as project management software, task lists, or calendar apps to help you stay organized and on track.
7. Set realistic goals: Set realistic goals that are achievable within a given timeframe. This can help you avoid overcommitting and feeling overwhelmed.

By improving your productivity, you can work more efficiently and effectively, accomplish more in less time, and achieve your goals with greater ease.

CHAPTER 5

Time Management

Time management is a critical aspect of working smart. Here are some tips to help you manage your time more effectively:

1. Set priorities: Set priorities based on your goals and objectives. This can help you focus on the tasks that have the greatest impact on your success.
2. Make a schedule: Make a schedule that includes your tasks, meetings, and appointments. This can help you stay on track and avoid procrastination.
3. Use a task list: Use a task list to keep track of your daily tasks and ensure that you are making progress towards your goals.
4. Break tasks into smaller pieces: Break larger tasks into smaller, more manageable pieces. This can help you avoid feeling overwhelmed and increase your motivation to get started.
5. Avoid multitasking: Avoid multitasking, as it can reduce your productivity and increase your stress levels.
6. Take breaks: Take regular breaks to help you maintain focus and avoid burnout.

7. Learn to say "no": Learn to say "no" to requests or commitments that do not align with your priorities or goals.

By managing your time effectively, you can work more efficiently, accomplish more in less time, and reduce your stress levels. This can help you achieve your goals and succeed in your career or personal life.

Techniques for managing your time effectively

There are several techniques you can use to manage your time effectively. Here are a few examples:

1. Pomodoro Technique: The Pomodoro Technique is a time management method where you work in 25-minute intervals (called "Pomodoros") with short breaks in between. After four Pomodoros, take a longer break. This can help you break your work into manageable chunks and increase your focus.
2. Eisenhower Matrix: The Eisenhower Matrix is a tool for prioritizing tasks based on their urgency and importance. Tasks are organized into four quadrants: important and urgent, important but not urgent, urgent but not important, and neither urgent nor important. This can help you focus on the tasks that have the greatest impact on your goals.
3. Time blocking: Time blocking is a technique where you schedule blocks of time for specific tasks or activities. This can help you stay on track and avoid procrastination.

4. Batch processing: Batch processing is a technique where you group similar tasks together and complete them all at once. For example, you might batch process email responses or data entry. This can help you save time and increase efficiency.
5. Avoiding multitasking: Multitasking can reduce your productivity and increase your stress levels. Try to focus on one task at a time and avoid distractions.
6. Using a task list: A task list can help you keep track of your daily tasks and ensure that you are making progress towards your goals.

By using these techniques and finding the ones that work best for you, you can manage your time more effectively and accomplish more in less time.

Avoiding time-wasters and distractions

Avoiding time-wasters and distractions is a crucial part of managing your time effectively. Here are some tips to help you minimize distractions and stay focused on your tasks:

1. Turn off notifications: Turn off notifications on your phone and computer, or set them to silent mode. This can help you avoid distractions from social media, email, and other apps.
2. Close unnecessary tabs and windows: Close unnecessary tabs and windows on your computer to reduce visual distractions and increase your focus.
3. Use website blockers: Use website blockers to block access to social media, news websites, and other distracting websites during work hours.
4. Create a distraction-free work environment: Create a quiet and organized workspace that is free from distractions such as noise, clutter, or interruptions.
5. Use time tracking apps: Use time tracking apps to monitor how much time you spend on different tasks and identify areas where you can improve your productivity.
6. Prioritize tasks: Prioritize your tasks based on their importance and urgency, and focus on the most important tasks first. This can help you avoid wasting time on less important tasks.

7. Take breaks: Taking regular breaks can help you stay focused and avoid burnout.

By minimizing distractions and staying focused on your tasks, you can manage your time more effectively and increase your productivity.

Maintaining focus and concentration

Maintaining focus and concentration is crucial to working smart and boosting productivity. Here are some tips to help you stay focused and concentrate on your work:

1. Eliminate distractions: Eliminate distractions from your environment, such as noise, clutter, or interruptions. This can help you stay focused on your tasks.
2. Practice mindfulness: Practice mindfulness techniques, such as deep breathing or meditation, to clear your mind and improve your focus.
3. Break tasks into smaller chunks: Breaking tasks into smaller chunks can make them more manageable and help you stay focused on the task at hand.
4. Use the Pomodoro Technique: The Pomodoro Technique, which involves working in short bursts of time, can help you stay focused and improve your concentration.
5. Take regular breaks: Taking regular breaks can help you avoid burnout and maintain your focus and concentration.
6. Get enough sleep: Getting enough sleep is crucial to maintaining your focus and concentration. Aim for 7-8 hours of sleep each night.

7. Exercise regularly: Exercise can help you reduce stress and increase your energy levels, which can improve your focus and concentration.

By practicing these tips and finding the ones that work best for you, you can maintain your focus and concentration and work smarter to boost your productivity.

CHAPTER 6

Automation and Technology

Automation and technology can be powerful tools for working smart and boosting productivity. Here are some ways you can leverage automation and technology to improve your work:

1. Use productivity apps: Productivity apps, such as project management tools, to-do list apps, and calendar apps, can help you stay organized and manage your time more efficiently.
2. Automate repetitive tasks: Automate repetitive tasks, such as email management or data entry, using software or tools that can perform these tasks automatically.
3. Use communication tools: Communication tools, such as instant messaging and video conferencing apps, can help you stay connected with your colleagues and work more efficiently.
4. Use collaboration tools: Collaboration tools, such as cloud-based document sharing and task management platforms, can help you work together with your team more effectively.
5. Leverage artificial intelligence (AI): AI-powered tools, such as chatbots or voice assistants, can help you automate tasks, provide support, and save time.
6. Use time-tracking software: Time-tracking software can help you monitor how much time you spend on different

tasks, identify areas where you can improve your productivity, and automate your billing and invoicing processes.

By leveraging automation and technology, you can streamline your work processes, automate repetitive tasks, and free up time to focus on more strategic or creative work.

Tools and software to automate and streamline tasks

There are many tools and software available to help automate and streamline tasks. Here are some examples:

1. Zapier: Zapier is a platform that connects over 2,000 apps and automates workflows between them.
2. IFTTT: IFTTT (If This Then That) is a free platform that enables users to create "recipes" that automate tasks between different apps and devices.
3. Trello: Trello is a project management tool that uses boards, lists, and cards to help you track tasks and collaborate with your team.
4. Asana: Asana is a task management tool that enables teams to manage projects, track progress, and collaborate in real-time.
5. Airtable: Airtable is a database management tool that combines the flexibility of a spreadsheet with the power of a relational database.
6. Evernote: Evernote is a note-taking app that enables users to capture and organize their ideas, notes, and to-do lists.

7. Google Drive: Google Drive is a cloud-based file storage and collaboration platform that enables users to store and share files, documents, and folders.
8. Hootsuite: Hootsuite is a social media management tool that allows users to schedule and publish content across different social media platforms.

By using these tools and software, you can automate and streamline your tasks, save time, and boost your productivity.

Integrating technology into your workflow

Integrating technology into your workflow can be a powerful way to work smarter and boost your productivity. Here are some tips for integrating technology into your workflow:

1. Identify areas where technology can help: Look for areas in your workflow where technology can help automate repetitive tasks or streamline processes. This could include tasks like data entry, email management, or scheduling.
2. Choose the right tools: Once you've identified areas where technology can help, research and choose the right tools to fit your needs. Make sure to choose tools that integrate with your existing workflow and are easy to use.
3. Set up integrations: To get the most out of your technology tools, set up integrations between different apps and software. For example, if you're using a project management tool, make sure it integrates with your calendar and email.

4. Customize your tools: Many technology tools allow for customization to fit your specific needs. Take the time to customize your tools to fit your workflow and preferences.
5. Train yourself and your team: Make sure to train yourself and your team on how to use the technology tools effectively. This can include providing tutorials, creating user guides, or offering training sessions.
6. Evaluate and adjust: As you integrate technology into your workflow, regularly evaluate how it's working for you and adjust as necessary. This can include identifying areas for improvement or tweaking your integrations.

By following these tips, you can integrate technology into your workflow in a way that boosts your productivity and makes your work more efficient.

Tips for using technology productively

Here are some tips for using technology productively:

1. Limit distractions: Turn off notifications for apps and social media platforms that are not work-related. Set specific times to check emails, messages, and social media.
2. Use productivity apps: There are several productivity apps available that can help you manage your time, organize your tasks, and stay focused. Some popular ones include Forest, Focus@Will, and RescueTime.
3. Utilize keyboard shortcuts: Keyboard shortcuts can save you time and effort. Learn the shortcuts for your most frequently used applications and tasks.

4. Use multiple monitors: Using multiple monitors can help you work more efficiently, as you can view multiple applications and windows at once.
5. Back up your work: Make sure to regularly back up your work to prevent losing important files and data.
6. Use the cloud: Cloud-based storage solutions like Google Drive and Dropbox allow you to access your files from anywhere and collaborate with others in real-time.
7. Take breaks: Taking short breaks can help you stay focused and prevent burnout. Use a timer to take a five-minute break every hour or so.
8. Keep your workspace organized: A cluttered workspace can be distracting and reduce productivity. Keep your workspace organized and free of clutter.

By following these tips, you can use technology in a way that boosts your productivity and helps you work more efficiently.

CHAPTER 7

Learning and Personal Development

Learning and personal development are essential components of working smart. Here are some tips for improving your learning and personal development:

1. Set learning goals: Set specific learning goals to help you focus your efforts and track your progress.
2. Seek out new knowledge: Seek out new learning opportunities by attending workshops, seminars, and online courses. Keep an open mind and be willing to try new things.
3. Read widely: Reading widely can expose you to new ideas and perspectives. Make a habit of reading books, articles, and blogs that are related to your industry or interests.
4. Network with others: Networking with others can help you gain new insights and perspectives. Attend industry events, join professional organizations, and connect with others on social media.
5. Practice new skills: Practice new skills regularly to help you develop your expertise and build your confidence.
6. Reflect on your learning: Take time to reflect on what you have learned and how you can apply it to your work. Keep a learning journal or take notes to help you remember important insights and ideas.
7. Set aside time for personal development: Set aside dedicated time for personal development. This could

include attending a yoga class, learning a new language, or pursuing a hobby.

By following these tips, you can improve your learning and personal development, which can help you work smarter and achieve your goals.

Importance of continuous learning and development

Continuous learning and development are essential for staying competitive in today's rapidly changing work environment. Here are some reasons why continuous learning and development are important:

1. Keeps you up-to-date: Continuous learning helps you stay up-to-date with the latest trends, technologies, and industry developments. This knowledge can help you make better decisions and work more efficiently.
2. Enhances your skills: Learning new skills and techniques can enhance your performance and make you more effective in your job. This can also make you more valuable to your employer and increase your career prospects.
3. Boosts your confidence: The more you learn and develop, the more confident you become in your abilities. This confidence can help you take on new challenges and achieve your goals.
4. Fosters personal growth: Continuous learning and development can foster personal growth and self-awareness. It can help you discover new interests and passions and lead to a more fulfilling life.

5. Improves your adaptability: Continuous learning can help you develop the ability to adapt to change and be more resilient in the face of challenges. This is a valuable skill in today's rapidly changing work environment.
6. Enhances your creativity: Learning new ideas and concepts can stimulate your creativity and inspire new solutions to problems.

By continuously learning and developing, you can stay ahead of the curve and achieve your full potential in your career and personal life.

Strategies for acquiring new skills and knowledge

Here are some strategies for acquiring new skills and knowledge:

1. Attend training and workshops: Attend training and workshops related to your field to learn new skills and techniques. This can be an effective way to learn from experts and stay up-to-date with industry developments.
2. Read books and articles: Read books, articles, and blogs related to your field to gain new knowledge and perspectives. This can help you learn new strategies and best practices that you can apply to your work.
3. Take online courses: Take online courses or attend webinars related to your field to learn new skills and gain new knowledge. There are many online learning platforms available today that offer a wide range of courses on various topics.

4. Find a mentor: Find a mentor who is experienced in your field and can provide guidance and advice on how to improve your skills and knowledge. A mentor can offer valuable insights and help you avoid common mistakes.
5. Practice regularly: Practice regularly to develop new skills and knowledge. The more you practice, the more comfortable you will become with the skills and techniques you are trying to learn.
6. Participate in networking events: Participate in networking events related to your field to meet other professionals and learn from their experiences. This can be a great way to gain new insights and ideas.

By using these strategies, you can acquire new skills and knowledge that will help you stay competitive and achieve your career goals.

Overcoming barriers to learning

Here are some common barriers to learning and how to overcome them:

1. Lack of motivation: It can be difficult to learn when you lack motivation. To overcome this, set clear goals for what you want to achieve, and find ways to make the learning process more enjoyable and engaging. Consider the benefits of learning and how it can help you achieve your goals.
2. Time constraints: Many people struggle to find the time to learn due to busy schedules. To overcome this, schedule dedicated time for learning and prioritize it over other

activities that are less important. Look for ways to make learning more efficient, such as listening to audiobooks or podcasts during your commute.

3. Learning style mismatch: Everyone has different learning styles, and it can be challenging to learn when the teaching method doesn't match your style. To overcome this, experiment with different learning styles and methods until you find what works best for you. Consider using visual aids, hands-on activities, or group discussions to help you learn.

4. Lack of resources: Limited access to resources such as textbooks or learning materials can make it difficult to learn. To overcome this, look for alternative resources such as online courses, educational videos, or library resources. You can also reach out to peers or mentors for recommendations.

5. Fear of failure: Fear of failure can be a significant barrier to learning. To overcome this, remind yourself that mistakes and failures are a natural part of the learning process. Focus on progress and improvement, rather than perfection. Embrace a growth mindset and see challenges as opportunities for growth.

By addressing these common barriers to learning, you can overcome obstacles and achieve your learning goals.

PARTIII

Cultivating Habits for Success

Cultivating habits for success involves developing routines and behaviors that help you achieve your goals. Here are some habits that can help you succeed:

1. Set daily goals: Start each day by setting specific, achievable goals that align with your long-term goals. This will help you stay focused and motivated.
2. Prioritize tasks: Identify the most important tasks and focus on completing them first. This will help you make progress toward your goals even when unexpected challenges arise.
3. Develop a morning routine: Establishing a morning routine can set the tone for your day and help you be more productive. Consider incorporating activities such as exercise, meditation, or journaling into your routine.
4. Practice self-care: Taking care of yourself is critical for success. Prioritize activities such as getting enough sleep, eating a healthy diet, and taking breaks to recharge.
5. Continuously learn and improve: To stay ahead of the curve, commit to continuous learning and improvement. This can include attending workshops, reading books, or seeking out mentors and coaches.
6. Practice time management: Effective time management is essential for success. Consider using tools such as calendars, to-do lists, and timers to help you manage your time effectively.
7. Embrace failure: Failure is a natural part of the learning process. Instead of fearing failure, embrace it as an opportunity to learn and grow.

By cultivating these habits, you can increase your productivity and success in all areas of your life.

CHAPTER 8

Mindset and Attitude

Mindset and attitude are crucial components of success. Here are some strategies for cultivating a positive mindset and attitude:

1. Practice gratitude: Regularly express gratitude for the people and experiences in your life. This can help shift your focus from what you lack to what you have, and promote feelings of contentment and fulfillment.
2. Develop a growth mindset: Embrace challenges as opportunities to learn and grow, rather than viewing them as threats. Adopt a growth mindset that values effort and persistence over innate talent.
3. Visualize success: Visualization can be a powerful tool for achieving your goals. Take time each day to visualize yourself succeeding, and focus on the feelings of accomplishment and satisfaction.
4. Practice self-compassion: Treat yourself with kindness and compassion, even when facing setbacks or failures. Acknowledge your limitations and mistakes, but don't let them define you.
5. Surround yourself with positivity: Surround yourself with people who inspire and motivate you, and limit exposure to negativity and criticism.
6. Practice mindfulness: Mindfulness can help you cultivate a greater sense of awareness and presence, and reduce

stress and anxiety. Consider practicing meditation or other mindfulness techniques.

By adopting a positive mindset and attitude, you can overcome obstacles, increase resilience, and achieve greater success in all areas of your life.

Cultivating a growth mindset

Cultivating a growth mindset is an important aspect of personal development and success. Here are some strategies for developing a growth mindset:

1. Embrace challenges: Instead of avoiding challenges, embrace them as opportunities to learn and grow. Embracing challenges helps you to develop a problem-solving attitude and build resilience.
2. Learn from failures: Failure is an inevitable part of growth. Embrace it as a learning opportunity and focus on the lessons learned. This will help you to develop resilience and an adaptive mindset.
3. Focus on effort over innate ability: Instead of focusing on natural ability, cultivate a mindset that values effort, persistence, and hard work. This will help you to develop a growth mindset that emphasizes learning and progress.
4. Celebrate progress: Celebrate small wins and progress. This will help you to stay motivated and maintain a positive attitude, even when facing setbacks.
5. View criticism as feedback: Instead of viewing criticism as a personal attack, view it as constructive feedback that can

help you to improve. This will help you to develop a growth mindset that emphasizes continuous improvement.

6. Surround yourself with growth-oriented people: Surround yourself with people who inspire and motivate you to grow and develop. This will help you to stay focused and motivated on your personal and professional goals.

By cultivating a growth mindset, you can develop the resilience, adaptability, and determination needed to achieve success in all areas of your life.

Developing a positive attitude towards work

Developing a positive attitude towards work is essential for success and fulfillment in your career. Here are some strategies for cultivating a positive attitude:

1. Focus on the positive: Rather than dwelling on negative aspects of your job, focus on the positive aspects. Think about the things you enjoy about your job, the skills you are developing, and the progress you are making.
2. Set achievable goals: Setting achievable goals can help you stay motivated and positive. When you achieve your goals, it will give you a sense of accomplishment and satisfaction.
3. Practice gratitude: Practicing gratitude can help shift your focus from negative to positive. Take time to appreciate the good things in your job, whether it's the support of your colleagues, the learning opportunities, or the compensation.
4. Cultivate a growth mindset: A growth mindset emphasizes learning and progress, which can help you maintain a

positive attitude towards work. Rather than viewing challenges as obstacles, see them as opportunities for growth.

5. Take care of yourself: Taking care of yourself can help you maintain a positive attitude towards work. Get enough sleep, exercise regularly, and eat a healthy diet. Take breaks when you need them, and engage in activities that help you recharge.

6. Surround yourself with positivity: Surround yourself with people who are positive and supportive. Seek out colleagues who are supportive, and avoid those who are negative or unsupportive.

By cultivating a positive attitude towards work, you can improve your job satisfaction, productivity, and overall well-being.

Overcoming negative self-talk and limiting beliefs

Negative self-talk and limiting beliefs can be major obstacles to developing a positive attitude towards work. Here are some strategies for overcoming them:

1. Identify negative self-talk and limiting beliefs: Start by becoming aware of your negative self-talk and limiting beliefs. Notice when you are being self-critical or when you have thoughts that limit your potential.

2. Challenge your negative self-talk and limiting beliefs: Once you've identified your negative self-talk and limiting beliefs, challenge them. Ask yourself if they are true, and look for evidence that contradicts them.

3. Reframe negative self-talk and limiting beliefs: Instead of focusing on the negative, reframe your self-talk and beliefs in a positive light. For example, instead of saying "I can't do this," say "I haven't figured out how to do this yet."
4. Practice positive affirmations: Positive affirmations are statements that help you shift your mindset from negative to positive. Repeat affirmations such as "I am capable," "I am worthy," and "I can succeed."
5. Surround yourself with positivity: Surround yourself with positive people and messages. Seek out colleagues who are supportive and uplifting, and expose yourself to positive affirmations and motivational materials.
6. Take action: Finally, take action to overcome your negative self-talk and limiting beliefs. Start by setting small goals that help you build confidence and gradually work your way up to larger goals.

By challenging negative self-talk and limiting beliefs, you can develop a more positive attitude towards work and achieve greater success and fulfillment in your career.

CHAPTER 9

Health and Wellness

Maintaining good health and wellness is essential for working smart and being productive. Here are some strategies for promoting health and wellness:

1. Exercise regularly: Regular exercise can improve your physical and mental health, increase energy and focus, and reduce stress. Find a type of exercise that you enjoy and make it a regular part of your routine.
2. Eat a healthy diet: A healthy diet can improve your mood, energy levels, and cognitive function. Aim to eat a balanced diet that includes fruits, vegetables, whole grains, lean protein, and healthy fats.
3. Get enough sleep: Adequate sleep is essential for cognitive function, mood, and overall health. Aim to get 7-8 hours of sleep per night and establish a regular sleep schedule.
4. Manage stress: Stress can have a negative impact on your health and productivity. Find healthy ways to manage stress such as exercise, meditation, or talking to a therapist.
5. Take breaks: Taking regular breaks throughout the day can improve productivity and reduce stress. Take a short walk, meditate, or simply step away from your work for a few minutes.
6. Stay hydrated: Drinking enough water can improve energy levels, focus, and overall health. Aim to drink at least 8 glasses of water per day.

By prioritizing your health and wellness, you can improve your productivity and work smarter, not harder.

Importance of taking care of your physical and mental health

Taking care of your physical and mental health is crucial for a successful and fulfilling life. Here are some reasons why it's important:

1. Improved productivity: When you take care of your physical and mental health, you can improve your productivity and performance at work or school. By maintaining a healthy lifestyle, you can have more energy, focus, and concentration to tackle your tasks.
2. Better mood and mental health: Good physical health can help to improve your mood and reduce symptoms of depression and anxiety. When you're in a positive mental state, you're more likely to be productive and successful.
3. Reduced stress: Taking care of your physical and mental health can help you manage stress and cope with difficult situations. Exercise, meditation, and other stress-reducing activities can help to lower cortisol levels and reduce the risk of burnout.
4. Increased longevity: Maintaining good physical and mental health can increase your life expectancy and reduce the risk of chronic illnesses such as heart disease, diabetes, and cancer.
5. Better relationships: Good physical and mental health can improve your relationships with others. When you're

feeling your best, you're more likely to have positive interactions with friends, family, and colleagues.

In summary, taking care of your physical and mental health is essential for a successful and fulfilling life. By prioritizing your health, you can improve your productivity, mood, relationships, and overall well-being.

Strategies for improving your diet and exercise

Here are some strategies for improving your diet and exercise:

1. Create a meal plan: Plan your meals for the week ahead of time to ensure that you're eating a balanced diet with plenty of fruits, vegetables, whole grains, lean protein, and healthy fats. This can also help you save time and money by avoiding impulsive and unhealthy food choices.
2. Stay hydrated: Drinking plenty of water can help to keep your body functioning properly and prevent dehydration. Try to drink at least 8 cups of water per day and limit your intake of sugary drinks like soda and juice.
3. Incorporate exercise into your routine: Regular exercise can help to improve your mood, reduce stress, and boost your overall health. Aim for at least 30 minutes of moderate

exercise, such as brisk walking or cycling, most days of the week.

4. Find an exercise buddy: Working out with a friend or family member can help to keep you accountable and motivated to stick to your exercise routine.

5. Limit processed foods and sugar: Processed foods and sugary snacks can contribute to weight gain and other health problems. Try to limit your intake of these foods and opt for whole, nutrient-dense foods instead.

6. Get enough sleep: Getting enough sleep is crucial for maintaining good health and energy levels. Aim for 7-8 hours of sleep per night and establish a regular sleep routine to help you fall asleep and wake up at the same time every day.

By following these strategies, you can improve your diet and exercise habits and achieve better physical and mental health.

Techniques for managing stress and preventing burnout

Here are some techniques for managing stress and preventing burnout:

1. Prioritize self-care: Make time for activities that help you relax and recharge, such as reading, meditation, or taking a hot bath.

2. Set boundaries: Learn to say "no" to requests that are not essential or that exceed your capacity, and delegate tasks when possible.

3. Practice time-management techniques: Prioritize your most important tasks and use time-management techniques like the Pomodoro Technique to stay focused and avoid procrastination.
4. Take breaks: Schedule regular breaks throughout your day, even if it's just a short walk or a few minutes of deep breathing.
5. Seek support: Reach out to friends, family, or a mental health professional if you're feeling overwhelmed or stressed.
6. Practice mindfulness: Pay attention to your thoughts and feelings in the present moment without judgment, and use techniques like deep breathing or visualization to help you relax.
7. Exercise: Regular exercise can help reduce stress and improve your overall health.
8. Take time off: Take regular vacations or time off work to help prevent burnout and recharge your batteries.

By incorporating these techniques into your daily routine, you can manage stress more effectively and prevent burnout, allowing you to be more productive and enjoy a better quality of life.

CHAPTER 10

Building Relationships

Building relationships is an important part of working smart, as it can help you achieve your goals more effectively and create a supportive network of colleagues and mentors. Here are some strategies for building relationships:

1. Be approachable: Smile, make eye contact, and be open to meeting new people.
2. Be a good listener: Show interest in what others have to say and actively listen to their perspectives.
3. Offer help and support: Be willing to lend a hand when needed and offer support to colleagues and teammates.
4. Attend networking events: Attend professional events and conferences to meet new people in your field and expand your network.
5. Join professional groups: Join professional organizations or groups related to your field to connect with like-minded individuals and gain new insights.
6. Participate in team-building activities: Participate in team-building activities to build rapport and trust with colleagues and improve team dynamics.
7. Show gratitude: Express appreciation and gratitude for the contributions of others, and offer positive feedback when warranted.

By building strong relationships, you can create a support network that can help you achieve your goals and advance in your career.

Importance of networking and building relationships

Networking and building relationships are important for several reasons:

1. Opportunities: Building relationships with others can lead to new opportunities for career growth, job offers, and collaborations.
2. Knowledge sharing: By networking with others in your field, you can gain valuable insights and knowledge that can help you advance in your career.
3. Support system: Building relationships with colleagues and mentors can provide you with a support system to turn to when facing challenges or seeking guidance.
4. Increased visibility: Networking and building relationships can increase your visibility within your industry, which can lead to more opportunities for advancement and recognition.
5. Personal growth: Building relationships can help you develop stronger interpersonal skills and improve your ability to communicate and collaborate with others.

Overall, networking and building relationships can help you achieve your goals more effectively, expand your knowledge and skills, and create a support system that can help you navigate your career.

Strategies for building and maintaining professional relationships

Here are some strategies for building and maintaining professional relationships:

1. Attend industry events: Attend conferences, trade shows, and networking events to meet new people in your industry.
2. Connect on social media: Use social media platforms such as LinkedIn to connect with others in your field.
3. Volunteer: Participate in professional associations and non-profit organizations to meet others who share your interests and values.
4. Offer help and support: Be willing to help others with their projects and offer your support when needed.
5. Follow up: Follow up with new contacts after you meet them to stay in touch and build a relationship.
6. Personalize your communication: When you reach out to someone, personalize your communication to show that you value their time and attention.
7. Be respectful and professional: Treat everyone you meet with respect and professionalism, regardless of their position or status.
8. Maintain regular contact: Keep in touch with your contacts on a regular basis, whether it's through social media, email, or in-person meetings.

By consistently building and nurturing your professional relationships, you can create a strong network of contacts who can help you achieve your goals and advance your career.

Leveraging your network for success

Here are some ways to leverage your network for success:

1. Ask for advice and guidance: Reach out to your contacts for advice on career development, job search strategies, or industry trends.
2. Seek referrals and introductions: Ask your contacts for referrals to potential employers or introductions to influential people in your industry.
3. Collaborate on projects: Partner with your network on projects and initiatives to build stronger relationships and gain exposure to new opportunities.
4. Share knowledge and resources: Share industry news, best practices, and other resources with your network to establish yourself as a valuable contributor.
5. Attend events and participate in groups: Attend industry events, join professional associations, and participate in online groups to expand your network and build your reputation.
6. Say thank you: Express gratitude to your contacts for their help and support, and offer to reciprocate in any way you can.

Remember that networking is a two-way street - it's important to give as well as receive. By being an active participant in your network and building mutually beneficial relationships, you can position yourself for success in your career.

Conclusion

In conclusion, working smart is all about optimizing your productivity and achieving success with less effort. By setting goals, identifying your strengths and weaknesses, delegating and outsourcing, managing your time effectively, learning and developing new skills, cultivating habits for success, taking care of your health and wellness, and building strong relationships, you can work smarter instead of harder. This book provides practical strategies and techniques to help you drop the hard work and boost your productivity. By implementing these strategies, you can achieve your goals, advance your career, and live a more fulfilling life.

Summary of the book's content

The book "Working Smart: How to Drop Your Hard Work and Boost Productivity" provides a comprehensive guide to help individuals optimize their productivity and achieve success with less effort. It covers various topics such as understanding your work, defining your goals and priorities, identifying and prioritizing tasks, creating a schedule that aligns with your goals, identifying your strengths and weaknesses, delegating and outsourcing, improving your productivity, time management, automation and technology, learning and personal development, cultivating habits for success, taking care of your health and wellness, and building relationships.

The book emphasizes the importance of working smart over working hard and provides practical strategies and techniques to help readers achieve their goals, advance their career, and live a more fulfilling life. It emphasizes the significance of setting SMART goals, identifying tasks that can be delegated or outsourced, avoiding time-wasters and distractions, maintaining focus and concentration, integrating technology into your workflow, and cultivating a growth mindset. It also highlights the importance of taking care of one's physical and mental health and building strong professional relationships. Overall, the book provides valuable insights and actionable advice to help individuals work smarter and achieve their desired outcomes.

Final thoughts on working smart

Working smart is a crucial skill in today's fast-paced and competitive world. It involves setting clear goals, prioritizing tasks, managing time effectively, leveraging technology, developing new skills, and cultivating habits that support success. By working smart, individuals can achieve their goals more efficiently and effectively, while also maintaining a healthy work-life balance. The strategies and techniques outlined in the book "Working Smart: How to Drop Your Hard Work and Boost Productivity" can help individuals overcome common barriers to productivity and achieve their full potential.

Action steps for implementing what you've learned.

Here are some action steps you can take to implement what you have learned from the book "Working Smart: How to Drop Your Hard Work and Boost Productivity":

1. Define your goals and priorities: Take some time to reflect on what you want to achieve and prioritize your tasks accordingly.
2. Use the SMART goal-setting method: Make sure your goals are specific, measurable, achievable, relevant, and time-bound.
3. Identify your strengths and weaknesses: Conduct a personal SWOT analysis to identify areas where you excel and areas where you need improvement.
4. Delegate and outsource tasks: Identify tasks that can be delegated or outsourced and find the right people for the job.
5. Manage your time effectively: Use time management techniques such as the Pomodoro Technique, to-do lists, and prioritization to manage your time more efficiently.
6. Use technology to automate and streamline tasks: Use tools and software to automate repetitive tasks and streamline your workflow.
7. Continuously learn and develop new skills: Take courses, attend workshops, and read books to continuously improve your skills and knowledge.
8. Cultivate habits for success: Develop a growth mindset, maintain a positive attitude, take care of your physical and mental health, and build relationships with others in your field.

By implementing these action steps, you can work smarter, not harder, and achieve your goals more efficiently and effectively.

www.ingramcontent.com/pod-product-compliance
Lightning Source LLC
Chambersburg PA
CBHW071555080326
40690CB00057B/2580